THE OLD ENGLISH HOUND

THE MASTIFF

THE POETRY OF DOGS

The Painter and his Pug. *William Hogarth*

The
Poetry
of Dogs

edited by Samuel Carr

B. T. Batsford Limited · London and Sydney

First published 1975
Selection © Samuel Carr

ISBN 0 7134 2989 5

Designed by Alan Hamp
Filmset by Keyspools Ltd, Golborne, Lancs
Made and printed in Great Britain by
The Anchor Press, Tiptree, Essex
for the publishers B. T. Batsford Ltd
4 Fitzhardinge Street, London W1H 0AH
and 23 Cross Street, Brookvale,
NSW 2100, Australia

Contents

The Illustrations

87 Head of a Dog. From the drawing by Pisanello
   (*fl.* 1430–1455)
   Louvre, Paris: Cabinet des Dessins

The illustrations on the endpapers are after woodcuts by
Thomas Bewick (1753–1828) in his *History of Quadrupeds*,
1790.

D is for Dog, steadfast, honest, and true;
I hope he gets married to Pussy, don't you?

VICTORIAN ALPHABET BOOK

Introduction

Most poems about animals are bad poems. About dogs
especially the proportion of good poems to bad is small.
The reason is not far to seek. Few writers, indeed few people,
are able to see animals—dogs especially—as they are.
Sentimentality distorts the vision and the consequence is that
otherwise admirable poets, and Kipling is a case in point,
when they come to write of dogs produce work of
embarrassing falsity. In this collection the aim has been to
include only poetry which is true both to itself and to its
subject.

Cats more than dogs lend themselves to poetic fantasy.
There is no canine equivalent to the cat verse of William
Cowper, Edward Lear, T. S. Eliot or Stevie Smith; the
latter's poem about the pug, here reproduced, is a much
more realistic affair than those she wrote about cats.

The artists in their clear-sighted way have had less difficulty
in seeing and portraying dogs as they actually are. Even
Rosa Bonheur and Edwin Landseer, neither of them notably
unsentimental painters, represented dogs as dogs. To look at
The Old Shepherd's Chief Mourner may induce a certain
uneasiness which, however, would fall away if the sheepdog
were isolated from the unconvincing situation in which it
finds itself. For the rest, artists as diverse as Van Eyck and
Breughel, Piero di Cosimo and Velasquez, Toulouse-Lautrec
and Bonnard, have all been successful in distilling the
essentially canine element in the dogs which appear so much
more often than cats in their, and other painters' work.

The most famous dog in drama is certainly Launce's
'Crab' in *The Two Gentlemen of Verona*. For this reason, even
though he is apostrophised by his master in prose, it was felt
impossible not to represent him here.

Poems and pictures, it should be emphasised, are not
intended as more than complements. In their different ways
they indicate what the dog is like in himself and how he

appears in relation to man. If in the end the book is one which will appeal to the lover of dogs, of poetry and of painting—by no means always the same individual—then its editor will be well content.

———

The wild dog

The City Dog goes to the drinking trough,
He waves his tail and laughs, and goes when he has had
   enough.
His intelligence is on the brink
Of human intelligence. He knows the Council will give him
   a drink.

The Wild Dog is not such an animal,
Untouched by human kind, he is inimical,
He keeps his tail stiff, his eyes blink,
And he goes to the river when he wants a drink.
He goes to the river, he stamps on the mud,
And at night he sleeps in the dark wood.

STEVIE SMITH (1903–1971)

13

For a good dog

My little dog ten years ago
Was arrogant and spry,
Her backbone was a bended bow
For arrows in her eye.
Her step was proud, her bark was loud,
Her nose was in the sky,
But she was ten years younger then,
And so, by God, was I.

Small birds on stilts along the beach
Rose up with piping cry,
And as they flashed beyond her reach
I thought to see her fly.
If natural law refused her wings,
That law she would defy,
For she could do unheard-of things,
And so, at times, could I.

Ten years ago she split the air
To seize what she could spy;
Tonight she bumps against a chair,
Betrayed by milky eye.
She seems to pant, Time up, time up!
My little dog must die,
And lie in dust with Hector's pup;
So, presently, must I.

OGDEN NASH (1902–1971)

14

Gun-dog. *From an engraving after Philip Reinagle*

Incident

Characteristic of a favourite dog

On his morning rounds the Master
Goes to learn how all things fare;
Searches pasture after pasture,
Sheep and cattle eyes with care;
And, for silence or for talk,
He hath comrades in his walk;
Four dogs, each pair of different breed,
Distinguished two for scent, and two for speed.

See a hare before him started!
—Off they fly in earnest chase;
Every dog is eager-hearted,
All the four are in the race:
And the hare whom they pursue,
Knows from instinct what to do;
Her hope is near: no turn she makes;
But, like an arrow, to the river takes.

Deep the river was, and crusted
Thinly by a one night's frost;
But the nimble Hare hath trusted
To the ice, and safely crost;
She hath crost, and without heed
All are following at full speed,
When, lo! the ice, so thinly spread,
Breaks—and the greyhound, DART, is overhead!

From an engraving after C. O. Murray

Better fate have PRINCE and SWALLOW—
See them cleaving to the sport!
MUSIC has no heart to follow,
Little MUSIC, she stops short.
She hath neither wish nor heart,
Hers is now another part:
A loving creature she, and brave!
And fondly strives her struggling friend to save.

From the brink her paws she stretches,
Very hands as you would say!
And afflicting moans she fetches,
As he breaks the ice away.
For herself she hath no fears,—
Him alone she sees and hears,—
Makes efforts with complainings; nor gives o'er
Until her fellow sinks to re-appear no more.

WILLIAM WORDSWORTH (1770–1850)

The dog and the water-lily

The noon was shady, and soft airs
   Swept Ouse's silent tide,
When, 'scaped from literary cares,
   I wander'd on his side.

My spaniel, prettiest of his race,
   And high in pedigree,—
(Two nymphs adorn'd with every grace
   That spaniel found for me,)

Now wanton'd lost in flags and reeds,
   Now, starting into sight,
Pursued the swallow o'er the meads
   With scarce a slower flight.

It was the time when Ouse display'd
   His lilies newly blown;
Their beauties I intent survey'd,
   And one I wish'd my own.

With cane extended far I sought
   To steer it close to land;
But still the prize, though nearly caught,
   Escaped my eager hand.

Beau mark'd my unsuccessful pains
   With fix'd considerate face,
And puzzling set his puppy brains
   To comprehend the case.

But with a cherup clear and strong
   Dispersing all his dream,
I thence withdrew, and follow'd long
   The windings of the stream.

My ramble ended, I return'd;
   Beau, trotting far before,
The floating wreath again discern'd,
   And plunging left the shore.

I saw him with that lily cropp'd
   Impatient swim to meet
My quick approach, and soon he dropp'd
   The treasure at my feet.

Charm'd with the sight, 'The world,' I cried,
   Shall hear of this thy deed;
My dog shall mortify the pride
   Of man's superior breed;

'But chief myself I will enjoin,
   Awake at duty's call,
To show a love as prompt as thine
   To Him who gives me all.'

WILLIAM COWPER (1731–1800)

From a woodcut by Thomas Bewick

Foxhounds. *From engravings by George Stubbs*

At the meet
from: Reynard the Fox

The hounds drew round him on the green,
Arrogant, Daffodil and Queen,
Closest, but all in little space.
Some lolled their tongues, some made grimace,
Yawning, or tilting nose in quest,
All stood and looked about with zest,
They were uneasy as they waited.
Their sires and dams had been well-mated,
They were a lovely pack for looks;
Their forelegs drumsticked without crooks,
Straight, without over-tread or bend,
Muscled to gallop to the end,
With neat feet round as any cat's.
Great-chested, muscled in the slats,
Bright, clean, short-coated, broad in shoulder,
With stag-like eyes that seemed to smoulder.
The heads well-cocked, the clean necks strong,
Brows broad, ears close, the muzzles long,
And all like racers in the thighs;
Their noses exquisitely wise,
Their minds being memories of smells;
Their voices like a ring of bells;
Their sterns all spirit, cock and feather;
Their colours like the English weather,
Magpie and hare, and badger-pye,
Like minglings in a double dye,
Some smutty-nosed, some tan, none bald;
Their manners were to come when called,
Their flesh was sinew knit to bone,
Their courage like a banner blown.
Their joy to push him out of cover,
And hunt him till they rolled him over.

JOHN MASEFIELD (1878–1967)

Tracie

from: Hesperides

Now thou art dead, no eye shall ever see,
For shape and service, Spaniell like to thee.
This shall my love doe, give thy sad death one
Teare, that deserves of me a million.

ROBERT HERRICK (1591–1674)

To a black greyhound

Shining black in the shining light,
   Inky black in the golden sun,
Graceful as the swallow's flight,
   Light as swallow, wingèd one,
Swift as driven hurricane—
   Double-sinewed stretch and spring,
Muffled thud of flying feet,
   See the black dog galloping,
   Hear his wild foot-beat.

See him lie when the day is dead,
   Black curves curled on the boarded floor.
Sleepy eyes, my sleepy-head—
   Eyes that were aflame before.
Gentle now, they burn no more;
   Gentle now and softly warm,
With the fire that made them bright
   Hidden—as when after storm
   Softly falls the night.

God of speed, who makes the fire—
   God of Peace, who lulls the same—
God who gives the fierce desire,
   Lust for blood as fierce as flame—
God who stands in Pity's name—
   Many may ye be or less,
Ye who rule the earth and sun:
   Gods of strength and gentleness,
   Ye are ever one.

JULIAN GRENFELL (1888–1915)

Not for sale

from: John Brown's Body

There was a man I knew near Pigeon Creek,
Who kept a kennel full of hunting-dogs,
Young dogs and old, smart hounds and silly hounds.
He'd sell the young ones every now and then,
Smart as they were and slick as they could run.
But the one dog he'd never sell or lend
Was an old half-deaf foolish-looking hound
You wouldn't think had sense to scratch a flea,
Unless the flea were old and sickly too.
Most days he used to lie beside the stove,
Or sleeping in a piece of sun outside.
Folks used to plague the man about that dog,
And he'd agree to everything they said:
'No—he ain't much on looks—or much on speed—
A young dog can outrun him any time,
Outlook him and outeat him and outleap him;
But, Mister, that dog's hell on a cold scent,
And, once he gets his teeth in what he's after,
He don't let go until he knows it's dead.'

STEPHEN VINCENT BENÉT (1898–1943)

Sleeping Bloodhound. *Sir Edwin Landseer*

Dogs

When I was once a wandering man,
  And walked at midnight, all alone—
A friendly dog, that offered love,
  Was threatened with a stone.

'Go, go', I said, 'and find a man
  Who has a home to call his own;
Who, with a luckier hand than mine,
  Can find his dog a bone.'

But times are changed, and this pet dog
  Knows nothing of a life that's gone—
Of how a dog that offered love
  Was threatened with a stone.

W. H. DAVIES (1871–1940)

Pomeranian bitch and puppy. *Thomas Gainsborough*

Children of Charles I. *Sir Anthony van Dyck*

*Engraved on the Collar of a Dog, which I gave
to His Royal Highness*

I am his Highness' dog at Kew;
Pray tell me, sir, whose dog are you?

ALEXANDER POPE (1688–1744)

29

Lament of a poor blind

Oh what shall I do for a dog?
Of sight I have not a particle,
    Globe Standard, or Sun,
    Times, Chronicle—none
Can give me a good leading article.

A Mastiff once led me about,
But people appeared so to fear him—
    I might have got pence
    Without his defence,
But Charity would not come near him.

A Bloodhound was not much amiss,
But instinct at last got the upper;
    And tracking Bill Soames
    And thieves to their homes,
I never could get home to supper.

A Foxhound once served me as guide,
A good one at hill, and at valley;
    But day after day
    He led me astray,
To follow a milk-woman's tally.

A Turnspit once did me good turns
At going and crossing and stopping;
    Till one day his breed
    Went off at full speed
To spit at a great fire in Wapping.

A Pointer once pointed my way,
But did not turn out quite so pleasant,
    Each hour I'd stop
    At a poulterer's shop
To point at a very high pheasant.

A Pug did not suit me at all;
The feature unluckily rose up,
    And folks took offence
    When offering pence
Because of his turning his nose up.

A butcher once gave me a dog,
That turn'd out the worst one of any;
    A Bull-dog's own pup,
    I got a toss up,
Before he had brought me a penny.

My next was a Westminster dog,
From Aistop the regular cadger;
    But, sightless, I saw
    He never would draw
A blind man as well as a badger.

A Greyhound I got by a swop,
But Lord, we soon came to divorces;
    He treated my strip
    Of cord, like a slip,
And left me to go my own courses.

A Poodle once towed me along,
But always we came to one harbour,
    To keep his curls smart,
    And shave his hind part,
He constantly called on a barber.

My next was a Newfoundland brute,
As big as a calf fit for slaughter;
    But my old cataract
    So truly he backed
I always fell into the water.

I once had a Sheep-dog for guide,
His worth did not value a button;
    I found it no go,
    A Smithfield Ducrow,
To stand on four saddles of mutton.

My next was an Esquimaux dog,
A dog that my bones ache to talk on,
    For picking his ways
    On cold frosty days
He picked out the slides for a walk on.

Bijou was a lady-like dog,
But vexed me at night not a little,
    When tea-time was come
    She would not go home—
Her tail had once trailed a tin kettle.

From a woodcut by Thomas Bewick

I once had a sort of a Shock,
And kissed a street post like a brother,
    And lost every tooth
    In learning this truth—
One blind cannot well lead another.

A Terrier was far from a trump,
He had one defect, and a thorough,
    I never could stir,
    'Od rabbit the cur!
Without going into the Borough.

My next was Dalmatian, the dog!
And led me in danger, oh crikey!
    By chasing horse heels,
    Between carriage wheels,
Till I came upon boards that were spiky.

The next that I had was from Cross,
And once was a favourite Spaniel
    With Nero, now dead,
    And so I was led
Right up to his den like a Daniel.

A Mongrel I tried, and he did,
As far as the profit and lossing;
    Except that the kind
    Endangers the blind,
The breed is so fond of a crossing.

A Setter was quite to my taste,
In alleys or streets, broad or narrow,
    Till one day I met
    A very dead set
At a very dead horse in a barrow.

I once had a dog that went mad,
And sorry I was that I got him;
   I came to a run,
    And a man with a gun,
Peppered me when he ought to have shot him.

My profits have gone to the dogs,
My trade has been such a deceiver,
   I fear that my aim
    Is a mere losing game—
Unless I can find a Retriever.

THOMAS HOOD (1835–74)

Detail from The Vision of St Augustine. *Vittore Carpaccio*

Detail from The Death of Procris. *Piero di Cosimo*

The Prioresse's dogs

from: The Prologue to the Canterbury Tales

Of smale houndes had she, that she fedde
With rosted flesh, or milk and wastel-breed,
But sore weep she if oon of hem were deed,
Or if men smoot it with a yerde smerte;
And al was conscience and tendre herte.

GEOFFREY CHAUCER (1367?–1434)

Detail of an altarpiece. Marziale

Two dogs have I

For years we've had a little dog,
Last year we acquired a big dog;
He wasn't big when we got him,
He was littler than the dog we had.
We thought our little dog would love him,
Would help him to become a trig dog,
But the new little dog got bigger,
And the old little dog got mad.

Now the big dog loves the little dog,
But the little dog hates the big dog,
The little dog is eleven years old,
And the big dog only one;
The little dog calls him *Schweinhund*,
The little dog calls him Pig-dog,
She grumbles broken curses
As she dreams in the August sun.

The big dog's teeth are terrible,
But he wouldn't bite the little dog;
The little dog wants to grind his bones,
But the little dog has no teeth;
The big dog is acrobatic,
The little dog is a brittle dog;
She leaps to grip his jugular,
And passes underneath.

The big dog clings to the little dog
Like glue and cement and mortar;
The little dog is his own true love;
But the big dog is to her
Like a scarlet rag to a Longhorn,
Or a suitcase to a porter;
The day he sat on the hornet
I distinctly heard her purr.

Well, how can you blame the little dog,
Who was once the household darling?
He romps like a young Adonis,
She droops like an old mustache;
No wonder she steals his corner,
No wonder she comes out snarling,
No wonder she calls him *Cochon*
And even *Espèce de vache*.

Yet once I wanted a sandwich,
Either caviar or cucumber,
When the sun had not yet risen
And the moon had not yet sank;
As I tiptoed through the hallway
The big dog lay in slumber,
And the little dog slept by the big dog,
And her head was on his flank.

OGDEN NASH (1902–1971)

Detail of an engraving by William Hogarth

Argus greets Ulysses

from the Odyssey, *XVII, trans.* Pope

Thus, near the gates conferring as they drew,
Argus, the dog, his ancient master knew;
He, not unconscious of the voice and tread,
Lifts to the sound his ear, and rears his head;
Bred by Ulysses, nourished at his board,
But ah! not fated long to please his lord,
To him, his swiftness and his strength were vain;
The voice of glory called him o'er the main.
Till then in every sylvan chase renown'd,
With Argus, Argus, rang the woods around;
With him pursued the youth the goat or fawn,
Or traced the mazy leveret o'er the lawn;
Now left to man's ingratitude he lay,
Unhoused, neglected in the public way.

★   ★   ★   ★

He knew his lord—he knew, and strove to meet,
In vain he strove to crawl, and kiss his feet;
Yet (all he could) his tail, his ears, his eyes,
Salute his master and confess his joys.
Soft pity touch'd the mighty master's soul,
Adown his cheek a tear unbidden stole.

★   ★   ★   ★

The dog whom Fate had granted to behold
His lord, when twenty tedious years had roll'd,
Takes a last look, and, having seen him, dies;
So closed forever faithful Argus' eyes.

HOMER

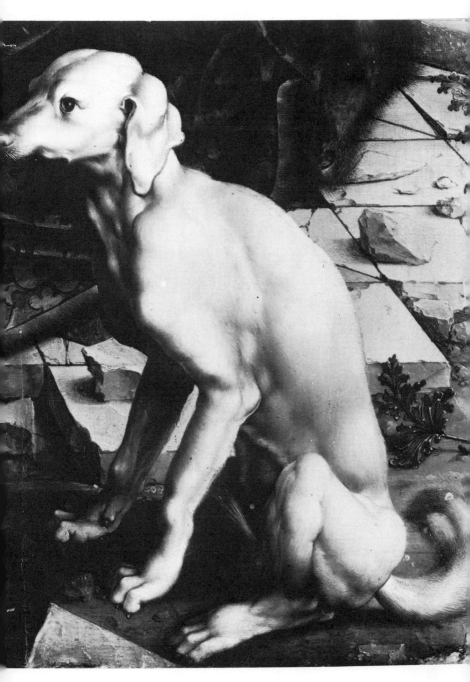

Detail from The Adoration of the Kings. *Jan Gossaert*

Cave Canem. *Roman mosaic*

42

Shepheard's dogge

from: The Shepheardes Calendar, *September*

Thilk same Shepheard mought I well marke;
He has a dogge to byte or to barke;
Never had shepheard so kene a kurre,
That waketh and if but a leafe sturre.
Whilome there wonned a wicked wolfe,
That with many a lambe had glutted his gulfe.
And ever at night wont to repayre
Unto the flocke, when the welkin shone faire,
Ycladde in clothing of seely sheepe,
When the good old man used to sleepe.
Tho at midnight he would barke and ball,
(For he had eft learned a curres call,)
As if a woolfe were emong the sheepe.
With that the shepheard would breake his sleepe,
And send out Lowder (for so his dog hote)
To raunge the fields with wide open throte.
Tho, whenas Lowder was farre awaye,
This wolvish sheepe would catchen his pray . . .
At end, the shepheard his practise spyed,
(For Roffy is wise, and as Argus eyed)
And when at even he came to the flocke,
Fast in theyr folds he did them locke, . . .
For it was a perilous beast above all,
And eke had he cond the shepherds call,
And oft in the night came to the shepecote,
And called Lowder, with a hollow throte,
As if it the old man selfe had bene.
The dog his maisters voice did it weene,
Yet halfe in doubt he opened the dore,
And ranne out, as he was wont of yore.
No sooner was out, but swifter than thought,
Fast by the hyde the wolfe Lowder caught;
And had not Roffy renne to the steven,
Lowder had be slaine thilke same even.

EDMUND SPENSER (1552–1599)   43

A dog's grave

My dog lies dead and buried here,
　My little Pet for five sweet years.
As I stand here, beside her grave,
　With eyes gone dim, and blind with tears—
I see it rising up and down,
As though she lay in a sleeping-gown.

Forgive me, Pet, that half these tears,
　Which make my eyes go dim and blind,
Should come from thoughts of love betrayed,
　When I had trust in my own kind:
And Christ forgive this living breath
That links such lives with my dog's death!

W. H. DAVIES (1871–1940)

44

To our house-dog Captain

Captain! we often heretofore
Have boxt behind the coach-house door,
When thy strong paws were rear'd against
My ribs and bosom, badly fenced:
None other dared to try thy strength,
And hurl thee side-long at full length,
But we well knew each other's mind,
And paid our little debts in kind.
I often braved with boyish fist
The vanquisht bull's antagonist,
And saw unsheath'd thy tiny teeth
And the dark cell that oped beneath.
Thou wert like others of the strong,
But only more averse from wrong;
Reserved and proud perhaps, but just,
And strict and constant to thy trust,
Somewhat inclement to the poor,
Suspecting each for evil-doer,
But hearing reason when I spoke,
And letting go the ragged cloak.
Thee dared I; but I never dar'd
To drive the pauper from the yard.

WALTER SAVAGE LANDOR (1775–1864)

Detail from 'Jan Arnolfini and his Wife'. *Jan van Eyck*

Elegy on the death of a mad dog

Good people all, of every sort,
  Give ear unto my song;
And if you find it wondrous short,
  It cannot hold you long.

In Islington there lived a man,
  Of whom the world might say,
That still a godly race he ran,
  Whene'er he went to pray.

A kind and gentle heart he had,
  To comfort friends and foes;
The naked every day he clad,
  When he put on his clothes.

And in that town a dog was found,
  As many dogs there be,
Both mongrel, puppy, whelp, and hound,
  And curs of low degree.

This dog and man at first were friends;
　　But when a pique began,
The dog, to gain some private ends,
　　Went mad and bit the man.

Around from all the neighbouring streets
　　The wondering neighbours ran,
And swore the dog had lost his wits,
　　To bite so good a man.

The wound it seem'd both sore and sad
　　To every Christian eye;
And while they swore the dog was mad,
　　They swore the man would die.

But soon a wonder came to light,
　　That show'd the rogues they lied:
The man recover'd of the bite,
　　The dog it was that died.

OLIVER GOLDSMITH (1728–1774)

Randolph Caldecott

The dog whose ears were cropt

'What have I done, to be thus mocked,
By my own lord and master docked?
Oh, the unspeakable disgrace!
To other Dogs how dare I show my face?
Ye Kings, nay rather tyrants of my race,
If such a trick were played on you . . . !'
Thus the young mastiff Towzer rent the skies
When with small heed for his shrill anguish'd cries
They seized his ears and shore them through.
He thought it was a loss: but as he grew
Found the advantage. He was born to fight,
And many a time would have come home at night,
When he had got the worst of matters,
With those appendages in tatters:
By the torn ear we know the quarrelling hound.

The less there is of one for foes to bite,
The better; and 'tis common sense,
Having one vulnerable ground,
To concentrate thereon our whole defence.
Thus Master Towzer, with his gorget round
His throat, and not a trace of ear
For Wolves to grab him by, had nought to fear.

LA FONTAINE (1621–1695)
    translated by Edward Marsh

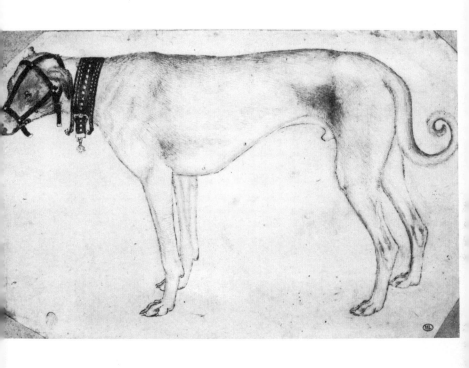

Muzzled Dog. *Pisanello*

Flush, or Faunus

You see this dog. It was but yesterday
I mused forgetful of his presence here
Till thought on thought drew downward tear on tear,
When from the pillow, where wet-cheeked I lay,
A head as hairy as Faunus, thrust its way
Right sudden against my face,—two golden-clear
Great eyes astonished mine,—a drooping ear
Did flap me on either cheek to dry the spray!
I started first, as some Arcadian,
Amazed by goatly god in twilight grove;
But, as the bearded vision closelier ran
My tears off, I knew Flush, and rose above
Surprise and sadness—thanking the true PAN,
Who, by low creatures, leads to heights of love.

ELIZABETH BARRETT BROWNING (1806–1861)

Miss Bowles. *Sir Joshua Reynolds*

Sheepdog trials in Hyde Park
for Robert Frost

A shepherd stands at one end of the arena.
Five sheep are unpenned at the other. His dog runs out
In a curve to behind them, fetches them straight to the
  shepherd,
Then drives the flock round a triangular course
Through a couple of gates and back to his master; two
Must be sorted there from the flock, then all five penned.
Gathering, driving away, shedding and penning
Are the plain words for the miraculous game.

An abstract game. What can the sheepdog make of such
Simplified terrain?—no hills, dales, bogs, walls, tracks,
Only a quarter-mile plain of grass, dumb crowds
Like crowds on hoardings around it, and behind them
Traffic or mounds of lovers and children playing.
Well, the dog is no landscape-fancier; his whole concern
Is with his master's whistle, and of course
With the flock—sheep are sheep anywhere for him.

The sheep are the chanciest element. Why, for instance,
Go through this gate when there's on either side of it
No wall or hedge but huge and viable space?
Why not eat the grass instead of being pushed around it?
Like blobs of quicksilver on a tilting board
The flock erratically runs, dithers, breaks up,
Is reassembled: their ruling idea is the dog;
And behind the dog, though they know it not yet, is a
  shepherd.

The shepherd knows that time is of the essence
But haste calamitous. Between dog and sheep
There is always an ideal distance, a perfect angle;
But these are constantly varying, so the man
Should anticipate each move through the dog, his medium.

The shepherd is the brain behind the dog's brain,
But his control of dog, like dog's of sheep,
Is never absolute—that's the beauty of it.

For beautiful it is. The guided missiles,
The black-and-white angels follow each quirk and jink of
The evasive sheep, play grandmother's steps behind them,
Freeze to the ground, or leap to head off a straggler
Almost before it knows that it wants to stray,
As if radar-controlled. But they are not machines—
You can feel them feeling mastery, doubt, chagrin:
Machines don't frolic when their job is done.

What's needfully done in the solitude of sheep-runs—
Those tough, real tasks—becomes this stylized game,
A demonstration of intuitive wit
Kept natural by the saving grace of error.
To lift, to fetch, to drive, to shed, to pen
Are acts I recognize, with all they mean
Of shepherding the unruly, for a kind of
Controlled woolgathering is my work too.

C. DAY-LEWIS (1904–1972)

Launce's dog, Crab

from: The Two Gentlemen of Verona

Launce.   When a man's servant shall play the cur with him,
look you, it goes hard: one that I brought up of a puppy;
one that I saved from drowning, when three or four of his
blind brothers and sisters went to it! I have taught him, even
as one would say precisely, 'thus I would teach a dog.' I was
sent to deliver him as a present to Mistress Silvia from my
master; and I came no sooner into the dining-chamber, but
he steps me to her trencher, and steals her capon's leg: O, 'tis
a foul thing when a cur cannot keep himself in all companies!
I would have, as one should say, one that takes upon him to
be a dog indeed, to be, as it were, a dog at all things. If I
had not had more wit than he, to take a fault upon me that
he did, I think verily he had been hanged for't; sure as I live,
he had suffered for't: you shall judge. He thrusts me himself
into the company of three or four gentlemanlike dogs,
under the duke's table: he had not been there—bless the
mark—a pissing while, but all the chamber smelt him.
'Out with the dog!' says one: 'What cur is that?' says
another: 'Whip him out,' says the third: 'Hang him up,'
says the duke. I, having been acquainted with the smell
before, knew it was Crab, and goes me to the fellow that
whips the dogs: 'Friend,' quoth I, 'you mean to whip the
dog?' 'Ay, marry, do I,' quoth he. 'You do him the more
wrong,' quoth I; ''twas I did the thing you wot of.' He
makes me know more ado, but whips me out of the chamber.
How many masters would do this for his servant? Nay, I'll
be sworn, I have sat in the stocks for puddings he hath stolen,
otherwise he had been executed; I have stood on the pillory
for geese he hath killed, otherwise he had suffered for 't.
Thou thinkest not of this now. Nay, I remember the trick
you served me when I took my leave of Madam Silvia: did
not I bid thee still mark me, and do as I do? when didst

Pablo Picasso

54

thou see me heave up my leg, and make water against a
gentlewoman's farthingale? didst thou ever see me do such
a trick?

WILLIAM SHAKESPEARE (1564–1616)

On a spaniel called Beau killing a young bird

A spaniel, Beau, that fares like you,
   Well-fed, and at his ease,
Should wiser be, than to pursue
   Each trifle that he sees.

But you have kill'd a tiny bird,
   Which flew not till to-day,
Against my orders, whom you heard
   Forbidding you the prey.

Nor did you kill, that you might eat,
   And ease a doggish pain,
For him, though chas'd with furious heat,
   You left where he was slain.

Nor was he of the thievish sort,
   Or one whom blood allures,
But innocent was all his sport,
   Whom you have torn for yours.

My dog! what remedy remains,
   Since, teach you all I can,
I see you, after all my pains,
   So much resemble man!

Beau's reply

Sir! when I flew to seize the bird,
   In spite of your command,
A louder voice than yours I heard
   And harder to withstand:

You cried—Forbear!—but in my breast
   A mightier cried—Proceed!
'Twas nature, Sir, whose strong behest
   Impell'd me to the deed.

Yet much as nature I respect,
   I ventur'd once to break
(As you perhaps may recollect)
   Her precept, for your sake;

And when your linnet, on a day,
   Passing his prison-door,
Had flutter'd all his strength away,
   And panting press'd the floor,

Well knowing him a sacred thing,
   Not destin'd to my tooth,
I only kiss'd his ruffled wing,
   And lick'd the feathers smooth.

Let my obedience then excuse
   My disobedience now,
Nor some reproof yourself refuse
   From your aggriev'd Bow-wow!

If killing birds be such a crime,
   (Which I can hardly see)
What think you, Sir, of killing Time
   With verse address'd to me?

WILLIAM COWPER (1731–1800)

Dog

O little friend, your nose is ready; you sniff,
Asking for that expected walk,
(Your nostrils full of the happy rabbit-whiff)
And almost talk.

And so the moment becomes a moving force;
Coats glide down from their pegs in the humble dark;

You scamper the stairs,
Your body informed with the scent and the track and the
    mark
Of stoats and weasels, moles and badgers and hares.

John Constable

We are going *Out*. You know the pitch of the word,
Probing the tone of thought as it comes through fog
And reaches by devious means (half-smelt, half-heard)
The four-legged brain of a walk-ecstatic dog.

Out through the garden your head is already low.
You are going your walk, you know,
And your limbs will draw
Joy from the earth through the touch of your padded paw.

Now, sending a little look to us behind,
Who follow slowly the track of your lovely play,
You fetch our bodies forward away from mind
Into the light and fun of your useless day.

    .   .   .   .   .

Thus, for your walk, we took ourselves, and went
Out by the hedge, and tree, to the open ground.
You ran, in delightful strata of wafted scent,
Over the hill without seeing the view;
Beauty is hinted through primitive smells to you:
And that ultimate Beauty you track is but rarely found.

    .   .   .   .   .

Home . . . and further joy will be waiting there:
Supper full of the lovely taste of bone.
You lift up your nose again, and sniff, and stare
For the rapture known

Of the quick wild gorge of food, then the still lie-down;
While your people will talk above you in the light
Of candles, and your dreams will merge and drown
Into the bed-delicious hours of night.

HAROLD MONRO (1879–1932)

59

To Flush, my dog

Darkly brown thy body is,
Till the sunshine, striking this,
  Alchemise its dulness,—
When the sleek curls manifold
Flash all over into gold,
  With a burnished fulness.

Underneath my stroking hand,
Startled eyes of hazel bland
  Kindling, growing larger,—
Up thou leapest with a spring,
Full of prank and curvetting,
  Leaping like a charger.

Leap! thy broad tail waves a light;
Leap! thy slender feet are bright,
  Canopied in fringes.
Leap—those tasselled ears of thine
Flicker strangely, fair and fine,
  Down their golden inches.

Yet, my pretty sportive friend,
Little is't to such an end
  That I praise thy rareness!
Other dogs may be thy peers
Haply in these drooping ears,
  And this glossy fairness.

But of *thee* it shall be said,
This dog watched beside a bed
  Day and night unweary,—
Watched within a curtained room,
Where no sunbeam brake the gloom
  Round the sick and dreary.

Roses, gathered for a vase,
In that chamber died apace,
  Beam and breeze resigning—
This dog only, waited on,
Knowing that when light is gone,
  Love remains for shining.

Other dogs in thymy dew
Tracked the hares and followed through
  Sunny moor or meadow—
This dog only, crept and crept
Next a languid cheek that slept,
  Sharing in the shadow.

Other dogs of loyal cheer
Bounded at the whistle clear,
  Up the woodside hieing—
This dog only, watched in reach
Of a faintly uttered speech,
  Or a louder sighing.

And if one or two quick tears
Dropped upon his glossy ears,
  Or a sigh came double,—
Up he sprang in eager haste,
Fawning, fondling, breathing fast,
  In a tender trouble.

And this dog was satisfied,
If a pale thin hand would glide,
  Down his dewlaps sloping,—
Which he pushed his nose within,
After,—platforming his chin
  On the palm left open.

This dog, if a friendly voice
Call him now to blyther choice
   Than such chamber-keeping,
'Come out!' praying from the door,
Presseth backward as before,
   Up against me leaping.

Therefore to this dog will I,
Tenderly not scornfully,
   Render praise and favour!
With my hand upon his head,
Is my benediction said
   Therefore, and for ever.

ELIZABETH BARRETT BROWNING (1806–1861)

From an engraving after C. O. Murray

Dulcina, a Bull-Terrier

Dulcina was, then suns rebelled
   And trod th'eternal work;
To every ball its limits held,
   The universe was stirred.

World embryons, in chaos rolled,
   Knew system at her cry,
And hoary planets ages cold
   Policed anew the sky.

Suns came and sun's star's satellites
   To sing Dulcina's power,
And myriad moons left myriad nights
   To keep a pagan hour.

In rebel red extravagance
   The flaming legions came;
In her transplendent brilliance
   They paled to candle flame,

And praised above all dams her dam,
   And gave her sire reward,
And hailed me blest o'er all who am
   Her bondsman and her bard;

Who sees in her all things glassed fair,
   And Paradise would fly,
That wanting her were angel-bare
   And drear felicity.

RALPH HODGSON (1871–1962)

Drink, puppy, drink

Hunting Song

Here's to the fox in his earth below the rocks!
   And here's to the line that we follow,
And here's to the hound with his nose upon the ground,
   Tho' merrily we whoop and we holloa!

   Chorus
   Then drink, puppy, drink, and let every puppy drink,
     That is old enough to lap and to swallow,
   For he'll grow into a hound, so we'll pass the bottle round,
     And merrily we'll whoop and we'll holloa.

Here's to the horse, and the rider, too, of course;
   And here's to the rally o' the hunt, boys;
Here's a health to every friend, who can struggle to the end,
   And here's to the Tally-ho in front, boys.
   Chorus

Here's to the gap, and the timber that we rap,
Here's to the white thorn, and the black, too;
And here's to the pace that puts life into the chase
    And the fence that gives a moment to the pack, too.
        Chorus

Oh! the pack is staunch and true, now they run from scent
        to view,
    And it's worth the risk to life and limb and neck, boys;
To see them drive and stoop till they finish with
        'Who-whoop'.
    Forty minutes on the grass without a check, boys.
        Chorus

G. J. WHYTE-MELVILLE (1821–1878)

The Beaufort Hunt. *James Seymour*

A popular personage at home

'I live here: "Wessex" is my name:
I am a dog known rather well:
I guard the house; but how that came
To be my whim I cannot tell.

'With a leap and a heart elate I go
At the end of an hour's expectancy
To take a walk of a mile or so
With the folk I let live here with me.

'Along the path, amid the grass
I sniff, and find out rarest smells
For rolling over as I pass
The open fields towards the dells.

'No doubt I shall always cross this sill,
And turn the corner, and stand steady,
Gazing back for my mistress till
She reaches where I have run already,

'And that this meadow with its brook,
And bulrush, even as it appears
As I plunge by with hasty look,
Will stay the same a thousand years.'

Thus 'Wessex'. But a dubious ray
At times informs his steadfast eye,
Just for a trice, as though to say,
'Yet, will this pass, and pass shall I?'

THOMAS HARDY (1840–1928)

Detail from The Adoration of the Kings. *Jan Gossaert*

The foxhounds

from: Reynard the Fox

But now the resting hounds gave cheer,
Joyful and Arrogant and Catch-him
Smelt the glad news and ran to snatch him:
The Master's dogcart turned the bend.
Damsel and Skylark knew their friend,
A thrill ran through the pack like fire
And little whimpers ran in quire.
The horses cocked and pawed and whickered
Young Cothill's chaser kicked and bickered
And stood on end and struck out sparks,
Joyful and Catch-him sang like larks.
There was the Master in the trap,
Clutching old Roman in his lap,
Old Roman, crazy for his brothers,
And putting frenzy in the others
To set them at the dogcart wheels,
With thrusting heads and little squeals.

JOHN MASEFIELD (1878–1967)

Huntsman and Dog. *Paolo Veronese*

69

O Pug!

To the Brownes' pug dog, on my lap, in their car,
coming home from Norfolk

O Pug, some people do not like you,
But I like you,
Some people say you do not breathe, you snore,
I don't mind,
One person says he is always conscious of your behind,
Is that your fault?

Your own people love you,
All the people in the family that owns you
Love you: Good pug, they cry, Happy pug,
Pug-come-for-a-walk.

You are an old dog now
And in all your life
You have never had cause for a moment's anxiety,
Yet,
In those great eyes of yours,
Those liquid and protuberant orbs,
Lies the shadow of immense insecurity. There
Panic walks.

Yes, yes, I know,
When your mistress is with you,
When your master
Takes you upon his lap,
Just then, for a moment,
Almost you are not frightened.

But at heart you are frightened, you always have been.

O Pug, obstinate old nervous breakdown,
In the midst of *so* much love,
And such comfort,
Still to feel unsafe and be afraid,

How one's heart goes out to you!

STEVIE SMITH (1903–1971)

Sir Edwin Landseer

72

Inscription on the monument of a Newfoundland dog

When some proud son of man returns to earth,
Unknown to glory, but upheld by birth,
The sculptor's art exhausts the pomp of woe,
And storied urns record who rest below:
When all is done, upon the tomb is seen,
Not what he was, but what he should have been:
But the poor dog, in life the firmest friend,
The first to welcome, foremost to defend,
Whose honest heart is still his master's own,
Who labours, fights, lives, breathes for him alone.
Unhonour'd falls, unnoticed all his worth,
Denied in heaven the soul he held on earth,
While man, vain insect! hopes to be forgiven,
And claims himself a sole exclusive heaven.
Oh man! thou feeble tenant of an hour,
Debased by slavery, or corrupt by power,
Who knows thee well must quit thee with disgust,
Degraded mass of animated dust!
Thy love is lust, thy friendship all a cheat,
Thy smiles hypocrisy, thy words deceit!
By nature vile, ennobled but by name,
Each kindred brute might bid thee blush for shame.
Ye! who perchance behold this simple urn,
Pass on—it honours none you wish to mourn:
To mark a friend's remains these stones arise;
I never knew but one,—and here he lies.

Newstead Abbey, November 30, 1808

LORD BYRON (1788–1824)

From an engraving after Philip Reinagle

74

Dog

Cock-a-doodle-doo the brass-lined rooster says,
Brekekekx intones the fat Greek frog—
These fantasies do not terrify me as
The bow-wow-wow of dog.

I had a little doggie who used to sit and beg,
A pretty little creature with tears in his eyes
And anomalous hand extended on his leg;
Housebroken was my Huendchen, and so wise.

Booms the voice of a big dog like a bell.
But Fido sits at dusk on Madam's lap
And, bored beyond his tongue's poor skill to tell,
Rehearses his pink paradigm, To yap.

However, Up the lane the tender bull
Proceeds unto his kine; he yearns for them,
Whose eyes adore him and are beautiful;
Love speeds him and no treason nor mayhem.

But, on arriving at the gap in the fence,
Behold! again the ubiquitous hairy dog,
Like a numerous army rattling the battlements
With shout, though it is but his monologue,
With a lion's courage and bee's virulence
Though he is but one dog.

Shrill is the fury of the proud red bull,
His knees quiver, and the honeysuckle vine
Expires with anguish as his voice, terrible,
Cries, 'What do you want of my twenty lady kine?'

Now the air trembles to the sorrowing Moo
Of twenty blameless ladies of the mead

Fearing their lord's precarious set-to.
It is the sunset and the heavens bleed.

The hooves of the red bull slither the claybank
And cut the green tendrils of the vine; his horn
Slices the young birch unto splinter and shank
But lunging leaves the bitch's boy untorn.

Across the red sky comes master, Hodge by name,
Upright, biped, tall-browed, and self-assured,
In his hand a cudgel, in his cold eye a flame:
'Have I beat my dog so sore and he is not cured?'

His stick and stone and curse rain on the brute
That pipped his bull of gentle pedigree
Till the leonine smarts with pain and disrepute
And the bovine weeps in the bosom of his family.

Old Hodge stays not his hand, but whips to kennel
The renegade. God's peace betide the souls
Of the pure in heart. But in the box that fennel
Grows round are two red eyes that stare like coals.

JOHN CROWE RANSOM (1888–1974)

The hounds of Theseus

from: A Midsummer Night's Dream

Hippolyta
I was with Hercules and Cadmus once
When in a wood of Crete they bay'd the boar
With hounds of Sparta: never did I hear
Such gallant chiding; for besides the groves,
The skies, the fountains, every region near,
Seem'd all one mutual cry: I never heard
So musical a discord, such sweet thunder.

Theseus
My hounds are bred out of the Spartan kind,
So flew'd, so sanded; and their heads are hung
With ears that sweep away the morning dew;
Crook'd-knee'd, and dew-lapt like Thessalian bulls;
Slow in pursuit, but match'd in mouth like bells,
Each under each. A cry more tuneable
Was never holla'd to, nor cheer'd with horn,
In Crete, in Sparta, nor in Thessaly;
Judge when you hear.

WILLIAM SHAKESPEARE (1564–1616)

Detail from Winter. *Jan Brueghel*

Detail from The Conversion of St Hubert. *Master of the Life of the Virgin*

78

The woodman's dog

from: The Task

Forth goes the woodman, leaving unconcern'd
The cheerful haunts of man; to wield the axe
And drive the wedge, in yonder forest drear,
From morn to eve his solitary task.
Shaggy, and lean, and shrewd, with pointed ears
And tail cropp'd short, half lurcher and half cur—
His dog attends him. Close behind his heel
Now creeps he slow; and now, with many a frisk
Wide-scamp'ring, snatches up the drifted snow
With iv'ry teeth, or ploughs it with his snout;
Then shakes his powder'd coat, and barks for joy.

WILLIAM COWPER (1731–1800)

Epitaph on Fop

A dog belonging to Lady Throckmorton

Though once a puppy, and though Fop by name,
Here moulders one, whose bones some honour claim;
No sycophant, although of spaniel race!
And though no hound, a martyr to the chase!
Ye squirrels, rabbits, leverets, rejoice!
Your haunts no longer echo to his voice.

This record of his fate exulting view,
He died worn out with vain pursuit of you.
   'Yes!' the indignant shade of Fop replies,
'And worn with vain pursuit, man also dies.'

WILLIAM COWPER (1731–1800)

from
A Book of Nonsense

There was an Old Man of Leghorn,
The smallest as ever was born;
But quickly snapt up he, was once by a puppy,
Who devoured that Old Man of Leghorn.

There was an old man of Ancona,
Who found a small dog with no owner,
Which he took up and down, all the streets of the town;
That anxious old man of Ancona.

EDWARD LEAR (1812–1888)

To a dog's memory

The gusty morns are here,
When all the reeds ride low with level spear;
And on such nights as lured us far of yore,
Down rocky alleys yet, and through the pine,
The Hound-star and the pagan Hunter shine;
But I and thou, ah, field-fellow of mine,
Together roam no more.

Soft showers go laden now
With odors of the sappy orchard-bough,
And brooks begin to brawl along the march;
The late frost steams from hollow sedges high;
The finch is come, the flame-blue dragon-fly,
The cowslip's common gold that children spy,
The plume upon the larch.

There is a music fills
The oaks of Belmont and the Wayland hills
Southward to Dewing's little bubbly stream,
The heavenly weather's call! O, who alive
Hastes not to start, delays not to arrive,
Having free feet that never felt a gyve
Weigh, even in a dream?

But thou, instead, hast found
The sunless April uplands underground
And still, wherever thou art, I must be.
My beautiful! arise in might and mirth,
For we were tameless travellers from our birth;
Arise against thy narrow door of earth,
And keep the watch for me.

LOUISE IMOGEN GUINEY (1861–1920)

BRIZC

Rosa Bonheur

Nino, the Wonder Dog

A dog emerges from the flies
   Balanced upon a ball.
Our entertainment is the fear
   Or hope the dog will fall.

It comes and goes on larger spheres,
   And then walks on and halts
In the centre of the stage and turns
   Two or three somersaults.

The curtains descend upon the act.
   After a proper pause
The dog comes out between them to
   Receive its last applause.

Most mouths are set in pitying smiles,
   Few eyes are free from rheum:
The sensitive are filled with thoughts
   Of death and love and doom.

No doubt behind this ugly dog,
   Frail, fairly small, and white,
Stands some beneficent protector,
   Some life outside the night.

But this is not apparent as
   It goes, in the glare alone,
Through what it must to serve
   Absurdities beyond its own.

ROY FULLER (1912–   )

Detail from Christ and the Money Changers. *Jacopo Bassano*

D is for Dog

My dog went mad and bit my hand,
  I was bitten to the bone:
My wife went walking out with him,
  And then came back alone.

I smoked my pipe, I nursed my wound,
  I saw them both depart:
But when my wife came back alone,
  I was bitten to the heart.

W. H. DAVIES (1871–1940)

From a drawing by Pisanello

87

Acknowledgements

The Publishers would like to thank the following for permission to include certain copyright poems:

W. H. Davies, *D is for Dog*; *Dogs*; *A Dog's Grave*. Copyright © 1963 by Jonathan Cape Ltd. Reprinted from THE COMPLETE POEMS OF W. H. DAVIES by permission of Mrs H. M. Davies, Jonathan Cape Ltd, London and the Wesleyan University Press, Connecticut

Jean de la Fontaine, *The Dog whose Ears were Cropt* (from THE FABLES OF JEAN DE LA FONTAINE, translated by Edward Marsh): William Heinemann Ltd, London

Roy Fuller, *Nino, the wonder dog* (from COLLECTED POEMS): André Deutsch Limited

Thomas Hardy, *A Popular Personage at Home* (from COLLECTED POEMS) (copyright © by Macmillan Publishing Co. Inc.): by permission of the Trustees of the Hardy Estate; Macmillan, London and Basingstoke; The Macmillan Company of Canada Limited; and Macmillan Publishing Co. Inc., New York

Ralph Hodgson, *Dulcina, A Bull-Terrier* (from COLLECTED POEMS): by permission of Mrs Hodgson, Macmillan, London and Basingstoke, and St Martin's Press, Inc., New York

C. Day-Lewis, *Sheepdog Trials in Hyde Park* (from THE GATE): by permission of the Executors of the Estate of C. Day-Lewis; Jonathan Cape Ltd, London and Harold Matson, Co. Inc., New York

John Masefield, Extracts from REYNARD THE FOX: by permission of The Society of Authors as the literary representatives of the Estate of John Masefield, and The Macmillan Publishing Co. Inc., New York

Harold Monro, *Dog* (from COLLECTED POEMS): Duckworth & Co. Ltd, London

Ogden Nash, *For a Good Dog*; *Two Dogs Have I* (from FAMILY REUNION): by permission of J. M. Dent & Sons, Ltd, London; and *Two Dogs Have I*—Copyright © 1948 by Ogden Nash, and *For a Good Dog*—Copyright © 1949 by Ogden Nash

John Crowe Ransom, *Dog* (from SELECTED POEMS): Gerald Pollinger Ltd, London; Random House, Inc., and Alfred A. Knopf, Inc., New York

Stevie Smith, *O Pug!*, *The Wild Dog*: James MacGibbon Esq., Literary Executor

While the Publishers have made every effort to obtain permission from the copyright holders of the poems and illustrations in this book, they would be most grateful to be told of any cases where an incomplete or incorrect acknowledgement has been made.

THE NEWFOUNDLAND DOG

THE SPRINGER, OR COCKER